WELCOME

Welcome to our celebration of the life, times and works of Colin Seeley, a man for whom the expression 'human dynamo' could've been coined.

He was a bundle of energy and enthusiasm who experienced huge highs and mighty lows, both professionally and personally, but who always projected a professional – and immaculate– appearance to the world.

This small appreciation tome has its basis in a magazine supplement produced to mark Colin's passing. That tribute has now been extended with more photographs and some additional text... but all of this still goes nowhere near giving the full picture of the extraordinary experiences of a man who lived a life less ordinary.

Colin's standing was exampled by the huge turnout at his funeral, held on February 10, 2020, at Eltham Crematorium, not far from his Bexleyheath birthplace, where hundreds congregated to listen to eulogies delivered and stories told, recognising a man who really, truly made his mark.

In this book, we've left out tonnes more than we've put in, but it has been a pleasure to compile, sorting through and

Colin Seeley, on the 500cc Ducati racer, pictured at Stafford in 2015.

researching a fascinating character. The archives of Mortons Media Group have given up numerous treasures, enabling a largely pictorial chronicling of Colin's motorcycling career. We hope you enjoy it.

James. **James Robinson.**

Pressing on, with Wally Rawlings over the back wheel, at Oulton Park in 1965. Just look at that inlet tract!

THE MAN

There are some people who've done little. There are some people who've done a lot. There are others who've done more than that. Then there was Colin Seeley. He'd done more than pretty much everyone.

Colin passed away just after his 84th birthday. He packed so much into his life, which began on January 2, 1936 when he was born in Kent, the only child of Percy and Hilda. They moved to Bexleyheath but then, when the Second World War broke out, Percy took a job in his native Suffolk, the family settling in the town of Brandon for the duration.

Hostilities over, the Seeley family returned to London, with Colin back at school—which he was to leave with no qualifications, though armed with a 'fair assessment' from his headmaster and a noted aptitude for things mechanical and metal-work.

His first job was with Harcourt motorcycles, in his native Bexleyheath, before working for numerous businesses, including Halfords. Young Colin passed his motorcycle test at the second attempt—much to his chagrin—on his father's Series A HRD Rapide and sidecar, which Percy trusted his teenage son to use as he wished.

Work took Colin to Schwieso, a motorcycle dealership with a sporting reputation, and while there he acquired the first motorcycle of his own—£10 worth of 250cc 1936 Velocette MOV, which came in boxes...

By now, Colin, who was already rebuilding motorcycles 'on the side,' wanted to work for himself and with the unwavering support of Percy and Hilda (who are pictured on the cover), in 1956 he opened his first business, in Belvedere. Colin had always wanted and planned to race (he'd had a one-off go in 1954 on a friend's BSA Star Twin) but never, until now, had the wherewithal. When a swinging-arm Triumph Trophy came his way, he started out enthusiastically, competing in scrambles, hill-climbs, grass track and even sprints on the all-purpose 500cc twin.

Business was going pretty well and by 1958 Colin had the agency for Matchless/AJS and was able to buy an ex-works 500cc Ajay scrambler, though it proved a fearsome beast, and he soon swapped to a 197cc Greeves—the Thundersley, Essex, concern was another agency he now held. On the little two-stroke he started to excel, and campaigned Greeves machines (a 250cc version followed the 197cc model) for the next couple of years.

Always a good talker, Colin at work on the Seeley stand; note the URS powered machine in the background.

Then in 1960, he decided it was time to go road racing... but not on a solo. In league with Wally Rawlings, who had been racing a solo and now worked for Seeley, they acquired a racing Manx Norton outfit, from no less a name than former world sidecar champion Eric Oliver. The Seeley/Rawlings duo made their debut on the Norton (which, in truth, was fairly worn out on acquisition and took a lot of fettling to get up to scratch) at Snetterton in 1960. From a field of 31, they placed 10th.

Next year, the call was made to switch to a Matchless outfit—a brand new G50, no less, was acquired and modified for sidecar racing, and aboard the single overhead camshaft single the team made its TT debut—a somewhat sensational sixth was the result, especially praiseworthy as they'd only taken part at a handful of meetings.

The 1962 TT was even better—see more of that further on—and that same season they were British sidecar champions. But the Matchless was struggling against the BMWs and for 1964 a Beemer was acquired; third in the world championship was the result, as well as a GP win in the Netherlands.

By 1965, manufacture had begun; again, you can read further about that later on in this book. Colin was still racing and doing well, coming third in the 1966 world sidecar title chase, though he was becoming increasingly busy; after finishing third at the 1967 TT, he called it a day on his own racing career. It was the

halcyon days of the Seeley G50/7R era. There were other interesting racing projects too—the URS four, QUB two-stroke, as well as Ducati's 500cc GP effort.

In 1971, he joined Bernie Ecclestone in his car racing effort; Seeley and Ecclestone had known each other for many years, back to the Harcourt/Bexleyheath days. Colin ended up involved in all manner of car racing enterprises, right up to Formula 1 level, where he ran the Brabham team in the 1980s.

Other projects in the same era included building various road and race bikes, with a variety of Japanese engines, the Phil Read Honda replica fours, as well as Honda's TL200E trials bike, under the 'Seeley International' banner. There was tragedy in the period though, with the death of Joan, Colin's first wife, who died in 1979. In her honour, Colin set up the Joan Seeley Memorial Trust.

After finishing with car racing in the 1980s, Colin was back in motorcycling in 1992—a year after he married Eva—running the Duckhams Norton BSB team for two-and-a-half years, then Castrol Honda, before two years with Ducatis. He joined auctioneer Bonhams as a consultant in 1999 and published a two-volume autobiography in 2006 and 2008.

During recent years, Colin Seeley had been a popular figure at classic events far and wide, often demonstrating period machines, eyes twinkling and lips smiling, enduringly positive, endearingly modest, and always full of enthusiasm. He pretty much did it all.

Colin Seeley and Wally Rawlings, in the 1962 Sidecar TT. They finished third.

SIDECAR RACING DAYS

Considering he'd only started racing sidecars in 1960, Colin Seeley's third place in the 1962 Sidecar TT was remarkable. What made it even more impressive is when one realises that during their debut season the Seeley team—the crewman being his long-time friend, colleague and associate Wally Rawlings—struggled to get an entry, only managing a small handful of appearances aboard the ageing, worn-out Manx Norton outfit they'd acquired from Eric Oliver, four-time sidecar world champion.

For 1961, Seeley changed tack, acquiring a brand new Matchless G50—he was an agent for the marque, so it made sense to race what he sold.

Matchless race shop chief Jack Williams was apparently somewhat aghast that one of his thoroughbred grand prix machines was going to be shackled to a chariot. The sidecar, incidentally, came from Canterbury, another firm which Seeley held the agency for.

With the bright red tanked 496cc single overhead camshaft Matchless delivered, Colin set about converting it for its new role—a conversion which, actually, didn't consist of that much at all. There was a 16 inch rear and an 18 inch front (only because Avon, with whom Colin was associated for tyre use, didn't make a suitable 16 inch front tyre), the front mudguard was removed and a sturdy brace applied to the front forks. Then the sidecar was welded on. And that, basically, was about it. Colin and Wally tested it, with trade plates, on the A2.

Despite the Seeley/Rawlings team's lack of experience, they were able to secure an entry for the 1961 TT races. The only

Hard-charging at Oulton Park, in 1963 on
the 650cc Matchless outfit. Regular rival
Chris Vincent, BSA, provides the opposition.

Matchless in the entry, they finished sixth, bested by four BMWs and the experienced Charlie Freeman, on his Manx Norton. It was a super impressive bow.

Sure, Colin was to go on and do better at the TT, finishing second in 1964, and in the same season winning the Dutch TT on the world stage, but by then he'd had two more years' experience, and was aboard the all-conquering BMW Rennsport. In 1962 he was aboard the single cylinder Matchless and was a relative novice, so the podium finish was all the more impressive and considering his later association with the Matchless engines in his own-made machines, this result seems very much more significant. He was also British sidecar champion the same year.

The next year, he was first non-BMW at the TT (in sixth place), but it was clear that he wasn't going to be able to beat them, so would have to join them. In 1964 he graduated to a BMW, which he raced for the next three years, including winning the 1964 Dutch TT, on his way to third in the world title chase, a result repeated in 1966. He kept the BMW for 'big' meetings, with a Norton Atlas outfit for domestic use. At the end of 1967, Colin called time on his own racing career in order to focus on business.

It wasn't until 1989 that Seeley had another try on a sidecar outfit—he'd not ridden a single sidecar since he'd stopped racing. And what did he make his return on? Well, a URS-powered outfit, which was to be the first kneeler he'd ridden and with the sidecar on 'the wrong side'. Still, he soon got the hang of it and became a regular, parading the three-wheeler—and others—in a spirited manner for the best part of the next 20 years.

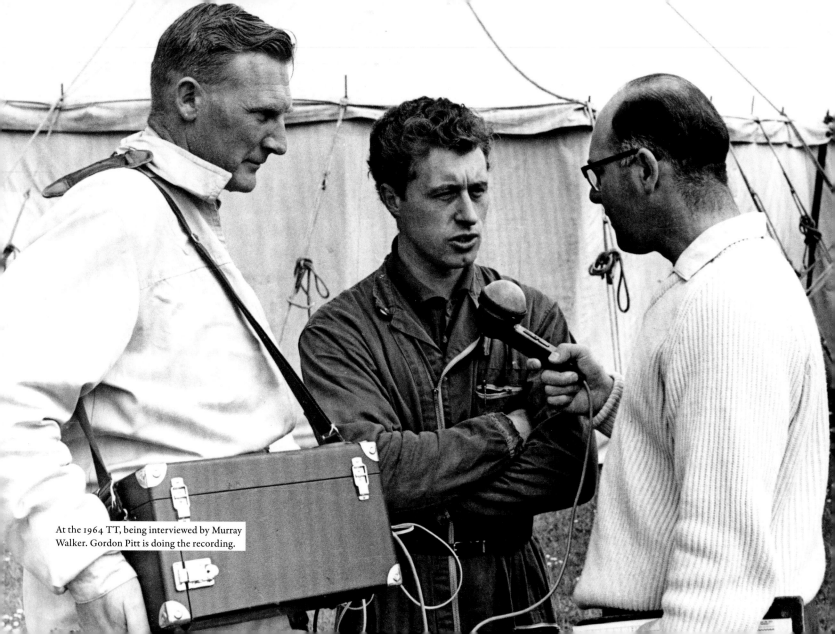

At the 1964 TT, being interviewed by Murray Walker. Gordon Pitt is doing the recording.

An early outing on the G50 at Crystal Palace, April 1961. Derek Yorke is chasing.

With Ken Sprayson at Oulton Park in 1964, discussing Matchless matters.

Partnered by Ray Campbell, 750cc
Dunstall Norton, at Snetterton in 1965.

Winning the 1964 Dutch TT aboard the FCS BMW, with Wally Rawlings in the chair.

Colin Seeley's last TT, the 1967 Sidecar race, with Ray Lindsey. They finished third.

Testing times, aboard the new Mk.II Seeley frame. Ron Chandler and John Cooper follow.

SEELEY G50

To classic enthusiasts, okay, the name Seeley is known for many things — from sidecar racing success through to the 1970s' Yamaha, Honda and Kawasaki powered machines, not to mention the Suzuki monocoque and much more besides.

But the 'classic' Seeley, the defining machine, is the Seeley G50, the 500cc racing machine that prolonged the life of the British single cylinder racer for longer than should've been possible.

The accompanying picture shows Colin leading Ron Chandler and John Cooper, through Paddock Hill bend, at Brands Hatch in February 1968. The occasion was the launch of the Mk.II frame, incidentally the one that Colin considered the best.

Talking to *Classic Racer* in 1999 he explained: "It was a big step forward because we went 1 1/8in, 17-gauge [Reynolds 531] tubing [from the original 1¼in 16-gauge) — it was a really nice frame. The Mk.II was difficult to get the engine in and out, but it's probably the one most people like."

The story of the Seeley G50 dates back to the winter of 1965/66, with the construction of the first Seeley frame. In the same *CR* article, Colin explained: "I tried to make my frames as simple as possible. Tie up the swinging arm point to the steering head as direct as you can — the more direct you can do that the better. Then you can put tubes all over the place.

"The first frame was really basic. I know I used a 27° head angle... I know I tried to make it right, to make it square. I was

With the Seeley 7R campaigned by John Cooper, Mallory Park, September 1968. Not long after, 'Coop' decided to install a Yamaha engine, to replace the 7R. On the Yamsel, John won 39 races on the trot, 150 in total.

always a stickler for getting everything in line, and it was very important to get the head right, not only the angle but also 90° to the swinging arm pick-up point. Otherwise the bloody thing would be out of line before you start."

But who to ride the first Seeley-framed racers? The answer came in the form of Derek Minter, renowned Norton ace but towards the twilight of his career. 'The Mint' rolled back the years and did what he did best, taking wins on both Seeley 7R (the identical-bar-capacity 350cc version) and the 500cc G50.

Despite the promising start, the relationship between Minter and Seeley wasn't altogether harmonious, and soon Minter went back to Norton, with John Blanchard taking over riding duties on the Seeleys. The new man finished fourth in the Senior TT race and came sixth in the 350cc race on the 7R for good measure.

At the end of 1966, Associated Motor Cycles (AMC) went into liquidation and Seeley bought all the G50, 7R and Manx Norton stock, rights, jigs, the lot. He was now a manufacturer 'proper'.

And there was good publicity coming too, as John Cooper — 'Mooneyes' — had been recruited and soon he was winning race after race on his Seeley G50, while Blanchard was still in the picture as well, with others also riding the Seeley machines. The Mk.II came in 1968, and it was on one that Dave Croxford was British 500cc champion.

The Mk.III chassis, designed by Eddie Robinson, responsible for the Seeley dual front brake (Colin started on a Vincent, remember) came in 1969 and then in 1970 the Mk.IV, with the straightest frame tubes of all and, like the Mk.III, devoid of a front downtube.

The Seeley G50 was to win lots of races and when classic racing took off, it became the machine to beat in that too, with Bob Heath taking a plethora of Classic Manx/TT wins aboard his example.

The first Seeley Matchless, pictured in March 1966.

Behind the counter. From left, it's
Arthur Keeler, Bill Wright and Colin.

The 500cc URS powered Seeley, pictured in July 1967. The engine, designed and made by sidecar ace Helmut Fath, was a big lump, but good enough to power John Blanchard to fourth at the Ulster GP.

Fettling a racer in April 1967.

Ron Chandler tries out the Seeley7R for size, with Colin behind.

Machines under construction in the Seeley race shop.

May 1966, Derek Minter in action on the 500cc Seeley G50.

Ron Chandler at the bottom of Bray Hill in the 1969 Senior TT, Seeley G50. He came sixth.

Mike Hailwood racing a Seeley
G50, at Mallory Park in 1969.

The almost-unbeatable combination of John Cooper and the Yamsel.

The road going Seeley Condor, with G50
Matchless engine. Colin on the left, and
that's Bernie Ecclestone in the middle.

The QUB (Queen's University Belfast) 500cc single, in a Seeley frame, 1970.

SEELEY HONDAS

There was no disputing the fact that the best motorcycle engines, the fastest and most powerful were, by the 1970s, coming out of Japan. The problem was though, the chassis lagged somewhat behind. In fact, quite a way behind, to the extent that some Japanese machines had downright scary reputations and nicknames to suit—'Widow Maker' anyone?

Seeley already had experience of Anglo-Japanese collaborations, going right back to when John Cooper and his 350cc Yamsel proved virtually unbeatable on the short circuits of the UK in the late 1960s. Other Japanese performance engines were duly fitted into Seeley frames, from Kawasaki and Suzuki, but these were largely 'unofficial' enterprises and always specialist racers.

During 1973 the Seeley business had endured a terribly tough time—there were a number of contributory factors (which including the fall in demand for G50 wares and the introduction of VAT, among other things) and there'd been a couple of dreadful years. But in 1975, Seeley were back in the motorcycle game.

The Honda CB750 was possessed of class-leading performance, but it was rather heavy. A new Seeley frame was developed to house the across-the-frame four, with a new frame in Reynolds 531 tubing leading to a weight saving of 10lb overall, with the Seeley Honda coming in a handy 23lb lighter than the standard CB750.

This new enterprise of Colin's was a stripped-back affair, a small team—originally just three—producing bespoke motorbikes. The new machine proved an immediate success, and soon

The initial Seeley Honda CB750, an initiative involving journalist David Dixon.

DIXON·SEELEY 812cc

it was being exported to the USA, Australia, South Africa and across Europe. Honda duly took note.

So much so, that when Honda decided to make replicas of Phil Read's TT winning Honda, Seeley was the man charged with the task of making the CB750 F2 look the part. It was simply a cosmetic affair, with a fairing, tank, seat, rearsets, suspension, exhaust system, handlebars and different tyres being the extent of the changes.

The plan was to make 400, but after 150 there was a fallout between Phil Read and Honda over licencing, leading to the model being rebranded as the Honda Britain SS model. This was to be made alongside the Seeley Honda, which sported Colin's own-made frame.

By now, Seeley and Honda were enjoying ever stronger links and so when Honda decided to build a trials bike, it was to Colin's firm they turned. A prototype was constructed and development riding undertaken by Trevor Kemp and former Scottish Six Days Trial winner Gordon Jackson, at Gordon's farm in Kent. When all were satisfied, the new model — tagged the TL200E (E for England) was displayed at the 1979 Earl's Court show, with orders taken for 100 units. There were further Honda projects too, including a revamp and 'improvements' to the CB750 model, in the form of fairing, side panels, silencers and other sundries.

Unfortunately, personnel changes meant that the Honda connection fizzled and ultimately ended, leaving Colin out of pocket and with a stock of unsold TL200Es, as the country plunged into recession. Colin was required to make another about turn, going into the retail business with the Seeley-Quik-fit Centre, supplying and fitting tyres, exhausts and such like to motorcycles. As ever, he set about the task with his customary zeal, soon establishing a successful enterprise.

Colin aboard the striking Seeley Honda.

The Seeley Honda
TL200E trials machine.

The undeniably handsome
Seeley Honda four.

Originally called the Phil Read Replica, a dispute led to later version of the Seeley-tweaked CB750 to be badged as 'Honda Britain.'

COLIN SEELEY

Old Forge Works, Stapley Road, Belvedere, Kent DA17 5JS Telephone No. 01 348-6006

Sales literature for the Seeley Honda.

TEAM MANAGER

It was in the middle of 1992 when the maverick engineer Brian Crighton, responsible for much of the development of the rotary Norton racer, posted an appeal in the press for assistance with his racing project.

By this point, Crighton had left the 'official' JPS-backed Norton squad and was running his own team, on a shoestring budget and called 'Roton racing'. Though it was all a somewhat haphazard affair, Colin could see the potential and relished the idea of a challenge. He contacted Crighton and, in double quick time, Colin was back in motorcycle racing.

In typical Colin Seeley fashion, he was like a terrier on a scent, immediately instigating a set of changes which, thankfully, Crighton and his band of loyal helpers could see the benefit of. In double-quick time, Roton was allowed to use the Norton name (which Colin realised was crucial to sponsorship, while the whole name situation was made stranger, as Crighton now worked for Norton again anyway, but on Drone engines) and Colin attracted a 'title sponsor' in the form of fuel company Duckhams. Loads of favours were pulled in, as sponsors were recruited, the team given a professional overall and a new, smart image, with a paint scheme in Duckhams' yellow-and-blue corporate colours. A good rider was required too; Ulsterman Mark Farmer was selected, and it was all systems go.

And 'go' the Farmer/Duckhams Norton did. Though the black-and-gold John Player effort was the official team, the sponsorship deal with the cigarette maker was already a year passed, it seemed people at Norton realised a back-up plan

Jim Moodie, hard-charging on
the Duckhams Norton in 1993.

might be sensible. And the Duckhams-backed crew proved its worth, while Steve Hislop—that year's Senior TT winner on a Norton—guested at a season-ending Brands Hatch race too.

But despite Colin's best efforts, finance was still a problem; Farmer was paid £150 a race weekend so, unsurprisingly, he chose to go elsewhere for 1993, which meant Colin needed a rider. He'd met Glaswegian Jim Moodie, a friend of Farmer's, and liked him; Colin probably saw something of himself in the wily, steely and determined racer. Jim, for his part, saw a good opportunity. He was largely magnificent, and although not winning any titles, he was second in the British Supercup championship, third in the ACU British Superbike championship and took 10 wins from 40 starts.

However, there wasn't any money to retain Moodie, so Seeley recruited hard-chargers Ian Simpson and Phil Borley who, although having both ridden 'big bikes', were arguably better known as 600cc campaigners. The Norton concern itself was imploding—Colin loaned £6000 to the team for essential new rotors to be made. Existence was seat-of-the-pants stuff (there were sometime 530 sponsors on the Norton) but the team looked uber professional—and, after a slow start to the season, delivered... and then some. Simpson became British Superbike champion, with teammate Borley third. From 65 races, the riders had 53 poles and 22 wins. In addition, on the Duckhams Yamaha, Simpson also took the 600cc Supersport title. It was a remarkable year, achieved on a shoestring.

After the Duckhams Norton days, the Seeley/Simpson/Borley triumvirate, along with the rest of the team, switched to be the official Castrol-backed Honda Britain team, racing the V-four RC45.

Though there were some highs, there weren't many; it wasn't like the old days, and the arrangement ended.

Colin then was reunited with Jim Moodie, alongside Ian Simpson, in an ill-fated Duckhams Ducati team, before a more successful 1997 managing the GSE Ducati team with Sean Emmett. A final season of management came in 1998, the Seeley Sport Supersport team running Colin's young Aussie protégé Karl Muggeridge. It laid the groundwork for Muggeridge, who became World Supersport Champion in 2004.

The winning combination of Ian Simpson
and the Duckhams Norton, 1994.

Colin at the
Louis Vuitton
concours event,
in 2002.

Colin is awarded his honorary membership of the AJS and Matchless owners' club by Roger Limb, in 2006.

Raising more money
for the Joan Seeley
charity, auctioning a
life-size Valentino Rossi
cut out in 2014.

Back where it all began — Colin reunited with father Percy's Series A Rapide, the machine Colin passed his test on, at Stafford in 2014.

Funeral and Celebration of the life of

Colin Jordan Seeley

2nd January 1936 – 7th January 2020

Eltham Crematorium
Monday 10th February 2020 at 12.30pm

Service taken by Celebrant Philip Painter

Eva, Joanne and Colin Jnr would like to thank you all for your presence here today and for your very kind thoughts and messages of sympathy and condolence.
You are invited for refreshments after this service at
The Foulston Suite
Brands Hatch Racing Circuit
West Kingsdown
DA3 8NG

Should you wish to make a donation in memory of Colin,
his family would ask you to support the work of:
The Joan Seeley Pain Relief Memorial Trust - 278697
30-90-76 - Account 01641810
or via www.justgiving.com/crowdfunding/colinseeley
Supporting and supplying specialist medical equipment to
hospitals and hospices across the UK